W9-BXN-293

WILD BACKYARD ANIMALS

Watch Out for MOUNTAIN LIONS!

Caitie McAneney

Peachtree

PowerKiDS press.

New York

Published in 2016 by The Rosen Publishing Group, Inc.
29 East 21st Street, New York, NY 10010

First Edition

Editor: Caitlin McAneney
Book Design: Katelyn Heinle

Photo Credits: Cover Volodymyr Burdiak/Shutterstock.com; back cover, pp. 3, 4, 6–8, 10, 12–14, 16, 18, 20, 22–24 (background) Polovinkin/Shutterstock.com; p. 5 Dennis W. Donohue/Shutterstock.com; p. 7 (map) Volina/Shutterstock.com; p. 7 (Florida panther) jo Crebbin/Shutterstock.com; p. 8 Jason Edwards/National Geographic/Getty Images; p. 9 creativex/Shutterstock.com; p. 10 anankkml/Thinkstock.com; p. 11 Drew Rush/National Geographic/Getty Images; p. 12 andy morehouse/Shutterstock.com; p. 13 (moose) Josef Pittner/Shutterstock.com; p. 13 (mountain lion) AppStock/Shutterstock.com; p. 13 (bighorn sheep) Michal Onderco/Shutterstock.com; p. 14 maZiKab/Shutterstock.com; p. 15 outdoorsman/Shutterstock.com; p. 17 welcomia/Shutterstock.com; p. 19 Anne Ackermann/The Image Bank/Getty Images; p. 21 Brandon Alms/Shutterstock.com; p. 22 Yair Leibovich/Shutterstock.com.

Cataloging-in-Publication Data

McAneney, Caitie.
Watch out for mountain lions! / by Caitie McAneney.
p. cm. — (Wild backyard animals)
Includes index.
ISBN 978-1-5081-4261-4 (pbk.)
ISBN 978-1-5081-4262-1 (6-pack)
ISBN 978-1-5081-4278-2 (library binding)
1. Puma — Juvenile literature. I. McAneney, Caitie. II. Title.
QL737.C23 M384 2016
599.75'24—d23

Manufactured in the United States of America

CPSIA Compliance Information: Batch #BW16PK: For Further Information contact Rosen Publishing, New York, New York at 1-800-237-9932

CONTENTS

A CAT OF MANY NAMES

Imagine you're out playing in your wooded backyard and suddenly you spot a big cat. It's nearly 5 feet (1.5 m) long with striking yellow eyes. It's a mountain lion!

There are many names for this big cat. Mountain lions are also known as pumas, cougars, panthers, and catamounts. Unlike the lions that rule the grasslands of Africa, these lions are found throughout the Americas. Let's explore more about the mountain lion!

MOUNTAIN LIONS ARE GREAT HUNTERS. LUCKILY, THEY DON'T WANT TO HURT HUMANS. THEY'D RATHER STAY FAR AWAY!

A MOUNTAIN LION'S HOME

Where might you spot a mountain lion? Mountain lions live in many kinds of **habitats**—from deserts to wetlands to forests. They're found across South America and Central America—from cold areas to **tropical** areas.

While mountain lions used to be found throughout the United States and Canada, they're now only found in the western part of North America. There's a small population of mountain lions living in Florida known as the Florida panthers. They're **critically** endangered, or at risk of dying out.

WHERE DID ALL THE MOUNTAIN LIONS GO? AS PEOPLE SETTLED ACROSS NORTH AMERICA, HUNTERS BEGAN KILLING THEM FOR SPORT. FARMERS AND RANCHERS HUNTED MOUNTAIN LIONS TO KEEP THEM FROM KILLING LIVESTOCK.

CANADA

UNITED STATES

ATLANTIC
OCEAN

MEXICO

CENTRAL
AMERICA

SOUTH
AMERICA

PACIFIC
OCEAN

MOUNTAIN LION
TERRITORY

BACKYARD BITES
Only around 100 adult Florida panthers exist, which makes them very **rare**.

FLORIDA PANTHER

IDENTIFYING A MOUNTAIN LION

How can you **identify** a mountain lion in your backyard? Mountain lions have tan fur and yellow eyes. They're around 3 to 5 feet (0.9 to 1.5 m) long, not including their tail. They weigh between 75 and 180 pounds (34 and 82 kg).

Mountain lions have strong back legs. They can jump up to 40 feet (12 m)! They can also leap into trees and climb over fences. They can run up to 50 miles (80 km) per hour for short periods of time.

BACKYARD BITES

Mountain lions have a great sense of sight. Like other cats, their pointed ears give them a great sense of hearing.

MOUNTAIN LIONS CAN CLIMB TREES AND ROCKY MOUNTAIN SLOPES. THEIR BODY HELPS THEM **ADAPT** TO NEARLY ANY HABITAT, INCLUDING BACKYARDS!

A HUNTER'S LIFE

Mountain lions are at the top of their **food chain**. They have a special way of hunting called ambush hunting.

As an ambush hunter, a mountain lion waits in hiding for its **prey**. Then, when the prey is in the right spot, the mountain lion strikes. It uses its powerful back legs to **pounce** on the animal. It attacks the prey from behind, ripping into the prey's neck with its teeth. The mountain lion holds on with its claws so the prey can't escape.

BACKYARD BITES

Mountain lions like to hunt alone at night. You may see them hunting just as the sun is rising or setting.

MOUNTAIN LIONS ARE SMART HUNTERS, TOO. WHEN THEY KILL A LARGE ANIMAL, THEY HIDE THE BODY UNDER DIRT AND LEAVES, AND EVEN UNDER SNOW. THEN, WHEN THEY'RE HUNGRY, THEY HAVE A MEAL WAITING.

TOP OF THE FOOD CHAIN

The mountain lion's amazing ambush skills and strong body make it a powerful predator. It'll eat nearly anything it can kill. A mountain lion will eat small animals, such as rabbits, raccoons, mice, and porcupines. It'll even eat coyotes, which are also great hunters.

Deer are one of the main parts of a mountain lion's diet. Deer are common, travel in herds, and are big enough to provide a lot of meat.

GRIZZLY BEAR

BACKYARD BITES

Mountain lions don't want to mess with wolves, grizzly bears, or black bears. A mountain lion might lose a fight to a predator like that!

THE BEST KILL FOR A MOUNTAIN LION IS A LARGE ANIMAL, SUCH AS BIGHORN SHEEP, MOOSE, OR ELK. THE MOUNTAIN LION CAN SAVE THE EXTRA MEAT FOR LATER.

BIGHORN SHEEP

MOOSE

LIFE CYCLE

Mountain lions are solitary animals, which means they like to live and hunt alone. However, a mother mountain lion will take care of her babies, called kittens or cubs, until they're around 18 months old.

Mother mountain lions usually give birth to around two to four cubs. They live together in a den. Baby mountain lions have blue eyes that turn yellow as they grow. They also have spots, which stay on their fur for around nine months.

WHEN A MOUNTAIN LION IS 18 MONTHS OLD, IT'S READY TO TAKE CARE OF ITSELF IN THE WILD.

BACKYARD BITES

Mountain lions live only around 10 years in the wild. Many are killed by predators when they're young.

MOUNTAIN LION ATTACKS

The good news is: mountain lions don't want to hurt people. In fact, they usually avoid people. However, there have been a few mountain lion attacks on people, and some were deadly.

In 2008, a 55-year-old man was attacked and killed by a mountain lion in Pinos Altos, New Mexico. Unlike attacks on hiking trails, this man was killed right near his home. As people build more houses on formerly wild land, the risk of crossing paths with a mountain lion increases.

THERE ARE ONLY AROUND FOUR MOUNTAIN LION ATTACKS EACH YEAR ACROSS THE UNITED STATES AND CANADA, AND MOST AREN'T DEADLY.

BACKYARD BITES

You can buy special fences to put around your backyard to keep mountain lions out. These fences should be high because mountain lions can jump!

SAFETY FIRST

Although mountain lion attacks are rare, it's smart to know what to do if you see one. Make sure you never walk alone in the wilderness, especially during the hours when mountain lions hunt. Pay attention to your surroundings—mountain lions are masters at hiding.

If you see a mountain lion, never run away from it. It may chase you. Instead, try to make yourself look bigger. Raise your arms, stand tall, and yell. Leave room for the mountain lion to get away.

IF YOU SEE A BEAR, IT SOMETIMES WORKS TO "PLAY DEAD" SO THE BEAR LEAVES YOU ALONE. NEVER ACT DEAD FOR A MOUNTAIN LION. SHOW IT THAT YOU'RE STRONG AND WILL PUT UP A FIGHT!

BACKYARD BITES

Keep your pets inside at night. A dog or cat might look like a nice meal to a mountain lion on the hunt.

AN ENDANGERED SPECIES

The mountain lion has a large **range** and great hunting skills. However, it's no match for humans. People construct buildings and roads in the mountain lion's backyard. Many are hit by cars as they try to cross roads.

Some mountain lions are killed out of fear if people see them in backyards or near towns and cities. Mountain lions have been killed for sport for hundreds of years. Farmers shoot mountain lions for killing livestock, even though most mountain lions leave livestock alone.

BACKYARD BITES

Even though mountain lions are endangered, it's not illegal to kill them. However, hunters need a special **license** to kill mountain lions.

THE MOUNTAIN LION HAS BEEN PUSHED FROM ITS HABITATS IN THE EASTERN PART OF THE UNITED STATES. NOW, THIS PREDATOR HAS TO FEAR HUNTERS AND CONSTRUCTION IN ITS ALREADY LIMITED RANGE.

A SOLITARY ANIMAL

Each year, thousands of mountain lions are killed and pushed farther out of their home range. But as solitary animals, these big cats just want to be left alone.

Mountain lions are important to their **ecosystems** because they keep populations of other animals under control. Without our help, mountain lions are at risk of dying out. It's important to educate people about this amazing animal. If you see a mountain lion in your backyard, just remember: that big cat just wants to hunt in peace.

GLOSSARY

adapt: To change to fit new conditions.

critically: Very seriously.

ecosystem: All the living things in an area.

food chain: A line of living things, each of which uses the one before it for food.

habitat: The natural home for plants, animals, and other living things.

identify: To tell what something is.

license: An official paper that gives someone permission to do something.

pounce: To jump suddenly toward or onto something.

prey: An animal hunted by other animals for food.

range: The area where something lives.

rare: Uncommon or special.

tropical: Warm and wet.

INDEX

WEBSITES

Due to the changing nature of Internet links, PowerKids Press has developed an online list of websites related to the subject of this book. This site is updated regularly. Please use this link to access the list: www.powerkidslinks.com/wba/lion